COOL SHOPS
NEW YORK

teNeues

Imprint

Editor: Desirée von la Valette

Editorial coordination: Michelle Galindo, Sabina Marreiros

Photos (location): Roland Bauer (192 Books, A Détacher, ABC Carpet & Home, Alexander McQueen, A.P.C., Apple Store Soho, Bagutta Life, BDDW, Bobby's Happy House, Bodum Cafe and Home Store, Boffi Soho, de Vera, Dean & Deluca, Fragments, Industries Stationery, Jeffrey, Kirna Zabête, La Perla, Malin+Goetz, Miya Shoji, MoMA Design and Book Store, Moss, MZ Wallace, Nakedeye, Polux Fleuriste, R by 45rpm, Rizzoli Bookstore, Sigerson Morrison, The Conran Shop, Xukuma), Courtesy Jonathan Adler (Jonathan Adler), Richard Davis (Comme des Garçons), Armin Linke (Prada New York Epicenter), Paul Warchol (Carlos Miele Flagship Store)

Introduction: Karin Mahle

Layout: Thomas Hausberg

Imaging & Pre-press: Jan Hausberg

Map: go4media. – Verlagsbüro, Stuttgart

Translations: SAW Communications, Dr. Sabine A. Werner, Mainz
Dr. Suzanne Kirkbright (English), Dominique Le Pluart (French)
Gemma Correa-Buján (Spanish), Elena Nobilini (Italian)

Produced by fusion publishing GmbH Stuttgart / Los Angeles
www.fusion-publishing.com

Published by teNeues Publishing Group
teNeues Publishing Company
16 West 22nd Street, New York, NY 10010, USA
Tel.: 001-212-627-9090, Fax: 001-212-627-9511

teNeues Book Division
Kaistraße 18, 40221 Düsseldorf, Germany
Tel.: 0049-(0)211-994597-0, Fax: 0049-(0)211-994597-40

teNeues Publishing UK Ltd.
P.O. Box 402, West Byfleet, KT14 7ZF, Great Britain
Tel.: 0044-1932-403509, Fax: 0044-1932-403514

teNeues France S.A.R.L.
4, rue de Valence, 75005 Paris, France
Tel.: 0033-1-55766205, Fax: 0033-1-55766419

teNeues Iberica S.L.
Pso. Juan de la Encina 2–48, Urb. Club de Campo
28700 S.S.R.R. Madrid, Spain
Tel./Fax: 0034-91-65 95 876

www.teneues.com

ISBN-10: 3-8327-9021-7
ISBN-13: 978-3-8327-9021-9

Contents

Introduction

More than in any other metropolis, a shopping excursion in New York is also an architectural experience. The design of the stores will often rival the merchandise they are supposed to sell. Most sales assistants know by now that "I'm just looking" can mean at the shelves as much as what is on them.

From the expensive boutiques on the Upper East Side to the smallest corner store, a strong concept with a matching design will find an audience, either to shop there or to marvel at the architect's, interior designer's or artist's creativity. Not long ago, store designers were looked down upon as decorators of temporary environments. Rem Koolhaas changed all that with his widely publicized Prada store. Now store design has become a fashionable way to show your design sensibility to a larger audience. But not only the stores by well-known designers are worth a visit. Sometimes it is the collaboration of an innovative client and a young designer that will yield the most astonishing results.

New York's most important contribution to the art of store design is the minimal aesthetic of the early Soho years. The clothing racks are placed like sculptures in an almost untouched loft to accentuate the industrial character of the space. A classic example is A.P.C. Or the original structure can be seen in a few places, as at Malin+Goetz. Another option is to create an environment for a brand that follows the same design direction as the merchandise such as in the Apple store, Bodum, Boffi or The Conran Shop.

You can go "shopping" here for days and never spend a dime. Whether it is a temple of cutting edge design or an insider's tip, *Cool Shops New York* will lead you to buys so exclusive, interesting and unusual that they will be hard to resist. Some memories you can take home in a shopping bag. Especially from the Big Apple.

Karin Mahle

Einleitung

Wie in kaum einer anderen Metropole ist in New York Einkaufen auch ein architektonisches Erlebnis. Die Gestaltung der Räumlichkeiten steht oft sogar gleichrangig neben der Ware, die es zu verkaufen gilt. In den meisten Läden haben die Verkäufer inzwischen verstanden, dass sich „I'm just looking" auch auf das Interieur und nicht nur auf die Ware beziehen kann. Von den teuersten Boutiquen an der Upper Eastside bis zu den kleinsten Eckläden, ein gutes Konzept mit einem entsprechend gestalteten Laden findet seine Liebhaber, sei es zum Einkaufen oder eben „nur" um sich an dem Einfallsreichtum von Architekten, Designern und Künstlern zu ergötzen. Noch gar nicht lange ist es her, da wurden Shop Designer eher mitleidig belächelt und ihre Arbeiten gerne als Dekoration von kurzer Dauer deklassiert. Spätestens nachdem Rem Koolhaas mit dem Prada Store auch in der Architekturszene Furore machte, ist diese Disziplin jedoch salonfähig geworden. Inzwischen gehört es zum guten Ton jedes Architekten und Designers, wenigstens einmal einen Laden gestaltet zu haben. Es sind jedoch nicht nur die von bekannten Größen entworfenen Geschäfte, deren Besuch lohnt. Oftmals ist es vielmehr die Kombination aus innovativen Unternehmern und gerade jungen Designern, die die aufregendsten Räume hervorbringt. New Yorks wichtigster Beitrag zur Ladenarchitektur sind die minimalistischen Läden und Galerien der frühen Soho-Ära. Leicht und ohne große innenarchitektonische Eingriffe werden die Kleiderständer wie Skulpturen in den Raum gestellt und man zeigt bewusst die Lagerhallenarchitektur. Ein klassisches Beispiel ist A.P.C. Oder man lässt die Struktur des Gebäudes nur an manchen Stellen durchscheinen, wie etwa bei Malin+Goetz. Oder aber das Raumkonzept wurde ebenso konsequent entworfen wie das Design der zu verkaufenden Ware, wie bei Apple, Bodum, Boffi oder The Conran Shop. So kann man tagelang „Einkaufen" gehen ohne auch nur einen Cent ausgeben zu müssen. Ob Designtempel oder Geheimtipp – die in Cool Shops New York vorgestellten Läden bieten immer auch exklusive, interessante und/oder originelle Waren, die zum Kaufen reizen. Denn Erinnerungen kann man auch in Einkaufstüten mit nach Hause nehmen. In Big Apple allemal.

Karin Mahle

6

Introduction

New York est l'une des rares métropoles où le shopping est aussi un plaisir architectural. L'aménagement des espaces est même souvent aussi important que les articles destinés à la vente. Dans la plupart des magasins, les vendeurs ont entre-temps compris que quand un client dit « I'am just looking », il peut aussi bien regarder les articles que la décoration.

Des boutiques les plus chères dans l'Upper East Side aux magasins d'angle les plus petits, un bon concept avec un magasin aménagé en conséquence trouve toujours des amateurs, que ce soit pour acheter ou « seulement » se délecter de l'extraordinaire imagination des architectes, designers et artistes. Il n'y a pas si longtemps, les shop designers suscitaient encore des sourires condescendants, et leurs travaux étaient rabaissés au rang de décorations vouées à l'éphémère. Cette discipline a fini par être acceptée, au plus tard, quand Rem Koolhaas a fait également fureur dans le milieu de l'architecture avec le Prada Store. Aujourd'hui, il est de ton bon que tout architecte ou designer ait réalisé au moins une fois l'aménagement d'un magasin. Mais il ne faut pas seulement aller visiter les magasins mis en scène par les plus grands du métier. En effet, les espaces les plus fascinants sont souvent le fruit de la rencontre d'entrepreneurs innovants et de jeunes designers.

Les magasins et les galeries minimalistes du début de l'ère de Soho représentent la contribution la plus importante de New York à l'architecture des magasins. Avec légèreté et sans grandes interventions sur l'architecture intérieure, les supports à vêtements sont placés dans l'espace comme des sculptures, et l'architecture d'entrepôt est délibérément montrée. A.P.C. en est un exemple classique. Ou on laisse seulement transparaître par endroits la structure du bâtiment, comme chez Malin+Goetz. Ou encore l'espace a été conçu de manière aussi systématique que le design de l'article à vendre, comme chez Apple, Bodum, Boffi ou The Conran Shop.

Ainsi on peut passer son temps à « acheter » sans devoir dépenser un seul cent. Que ce soit un temple du design ou une bonne adresse, les magasins présentés dans *Cool Shops New York* offrent toujours des articles exclusifs, intéressants et originaux qui incitent à l'achat. Et un souvenir, on peut l'emporter aussi dans un sac. A Big Apple, certainement !

Karin Mahle

Introducción

Más que en ninguna otra metrópolis, una excursión de compras en Nueva York es una experiencia arquitectural. El diseño de las tiendas rivaliza a menudo la supuesta mercancía de venta. La mayoría de los vendedores hasta ahora están concientes que "solo estoy mirando" lo cual significa al estante tanto como lo que esta en ellos. Desde las boutiques costosas en el área de Upper East Side hasta la más pequeña tienda de la esquina, con un concepto firme y la tienda decorada adecuadamente encontrara su auditorio; ya sea para comprar ahí o para admirar la creatividad de los arquitectos, diseñadores y artistas. No hace mucho, los diseñadores de tiendas eran solo reconocidos como decoradores de ambientes temporales. Rem Koohlhaas lo ha cambiado todo con la extensa publicación de la tienda Prada. Ahora el diseño de tiendas se ha convertido en una forma de moda para mostrar la sensibilidad de diseño a un auditorio más grande. No solo las tiendas por los diseñadores mejores conocidos merecen una visita. A veces es la colaboración de una innovadora clientela y un diseñador joven que dará los resultados más asombrosos.

Una de las contribuciones mas importantes de Nueva York para el arte de diseño de tiendas es la estética mínima de los primeros años del área de Soho. Los estantes de ropa y unidades de exposición son colocadas como esculturas en un desván casi intacto para acentuar el carácter industrial del espacio. Un ejemplo clásico es A.P.C. o como en otros lugares en donde la estructura original puede ser vista, así como en Malin+Goetz. Otra opción es crear un ambiente para una marca específica que siga la dirección del mismo diseño como la de la mercancía de venta, tal como la de la tienda Apple, Bodum, Boffi o The Conran Shop.

Puedes ir de "compras" aquí por días y nunca gastar ni una moneda. Ya sea en un templo de diseño de última moda o un lugar aconsejado; *Cool Shops New York* te guiara a compras exclusivas, interesantes e inusuales que serán difíciles de resistir. Algunas memorias te podrás llevar a casa hasta en una bolsa de compras, especialmente del Big Apple.

Karin Mahle

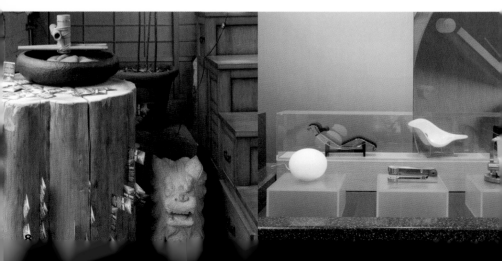

Introduzione

Fare compere a New York è anche un'esperienza architettonica: in questo la metropoli è pressoché ineguagliabile. L'arredamento degli ambienti assume spesso la stessa importanza della merce in vendita. Nella maggior parte dei negozi i commessi hanno ormai capito che la frase "I'm just looking", ovvero "sto dando solo un'occhiata", può anche essere riferita agli interni e non alla sola merce. Dalle boutique più care sull'Upper East Side ai negozietti più piccoli agli angoli, ogni ottima idea e il negozio che la concretizza trovano i propri amatori, sia per fare compere oppure, appunto, "solo" per dilettarsi con l'ingegnosità di architetti, designer e artisti. Non è passato molto tempo da quando gli *shop designer* venivano più che altro derisi compassionevolmente per i loro lavori spesso e volentieri declassati a decorazioni effimere. Dopo il furore suscitato da Rem Koolhaas anche nella scena architettonica con il Prada Store, tale disciplina è ora considerata un argomento degno di conversazioni all'interno della buona società. È ormai diventata una questione di bon ton tra architetti e designer aver progettato o arredato un negozio almeno una volta nella propria carriera. Non sono tuttavia solo i negozi progettati dalle celebrità a meritare una visita. Anzi spesso è la combinazione di imprenditori innovativi e giovani designer a dar vita agli ambienti più eccitanti.
Il contributo più importante che New York ha offerto all'architettura di negozi sono le gallerie e i negozi minimalisti della prima era Soho. Leggeri e senza grandi interventi di architettura interna, i portabiti vengono disposti nell'ambiente come sculture, e l'architettura dei capannoni viene consapevolmente mostrati. Un tipico esempio è A.P.C. Oppure si lascia trasparire la struttura dell'edificio solo in alcuni punti, come per esempio da Malin+Goetz. O, perché no?, gli spazi vengono progettati in maniera coerente con il design dei prodotti in vendita, come da Apple, Bodum, Boffi o The Conran Shop.
È possibile così "andare a fare compere" per giorni interi senza dover nemmeno spendere un centesimo. Che si tratti del tempio del design o di un consiglio chicca, i negozi presentati in *Cool Shops New York* offrono sempre anche articoli esclusivi, interessanti e/o originali che invogliano all'acquisto. I ricordi infatti si possono portare a casa in sacchetti della spesa. Nella Grande Mela di certo.

Karin Mahle

192 Books

Design: Richard Gluckman

192 10th Avenue | New York, NY 10011 | Chelsea
Phone: +1 212 255 4022
www.192books.com
Subway: C, E to 23rd Street
Opening hours: Tue–Sat 11 am to 7 pm, Sun–Mon 12 noon to 6 pm
Products: Books, artwork
Special features: Weekly readings

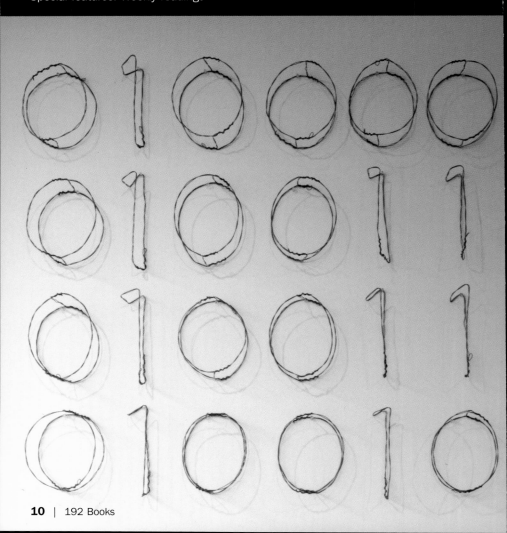

ABC Carpet & Home

Design: Paul Revere Williams

888 Broadway | New York, NY 10003 | Union Square | Flatiron
Phone: +1 212 473 3000
www.abchome.com
Subway: 4, 5, L, N, Q, R, W to Union Square, 6 to 23rd Street
Opening hours: Mon–Fri 10 am to 8 pm, Sat 10 am to 7 pm, Sun 11 am to 6:30 pm
Products: Carpets, furniture, accessories
Special features: Restaurants include: Pipa, Lucy and Le Pain Quotidien

262 Mott Street | New York, NY 10012 | Soho
Phone: +1 212 625 3380
Subway: B, D, F, V to Broadway-Lafayette Street
Opening hours: Mon–Sat 11 am to 7 pm, Sun 12 noon to 6 pm
Products: Fashion

Alexander McQueen

Design: William Russell, Alexander McQueen

417 West 14th Street | New York, NY 10014 | Chelsea
Phone: +1 212 645 1797
www.alexandermcqueen.com
Subway: A, C, E to 14th Street; L to 8th Avenue
Opening hours: Mon–Sat 11 am to 7 pm, Sun 12 noon to 6 pm
Products: Fashion, menswear, eyewear, perfume

Opening hours: Mon–Fri 11 am to 7 pm, Sun 12 noon to 6 pm
Products: Fashion

software

software

kids

EXIT

genius

genius

ipod

76 Greene Street | New York, NY 10012 | Soho
Phone: +1 212 925 5216
www.baguttalife.com
Subway: N, R to Greene Street
Opening hours: Mon–Sat 11 am to 7 pm, Sun 12 noon to 6:30 pm
Products: Fashion clothing; Prada, Dior, Galliano, Marni, Cavalli

BDDW

Design: Tyler Hays

5 Crosby Street | New York, NY 10013 | Soho
Phone: +1 212 625 1230
www.bddw.com
Subway: 6, J, M, N, Q, R, W, Z to Canal Street
Opening hours: Mon appointment only, Tue–Fri 10 am to 6 pm, Sat 12 noon to 6 pm,
Sun closed
Products: Handmade furniture
Special features: Handmade American furniture – traditional wood-working with modern
sensibility

Bobby's Happy House

2335 8th Avenue | New York, NY 10027 | Harlem
Phone: +1 212 633 5240
Subway: A, B, C, D to 125th Street
Opening hours: Mon–Sat 11 am to 7 pm, Sun 12 noon to 6 pm
Products: Records

Bodum Cafe and Home Store

413–415 West 14th Street | New York, NY 10014 | Chelsea
Phone: +1 212 367 9125
www.bodum.com
Subway: A, C, E to 14th Street; L to Eighth Avenue
Opening hours: Mon–Sat 10 am to 7 pm, Sun 12 noon to 6 pm
Products: Kitchenware and home accessories

Boffi Soho

Design: Piero Lissoni

31 1/2 Greene Street | New York, NY 10013 | Soho
Phone: +1 212 431 8282
www.boffisoho.com
Subway: 6, J, M, N, Q, R, W, Z to Canal Street
Opening hours: Tue–Fri 11 am to 7 pm, Sat 12 noon to 7 pm
Products: Kitchens, bathrooms, home

Carlos Miele Flagship Store

Design: Hani Rashid and Lise Anne Couture of Asymptote

408 West 14th Street | New York, NY 10014 | Meatpacking District
Phone: +1 646 336 6642
www.carlosmiele.com.br
Subway: A, C, E to 14th Street
Opening hours: Mon–Sat 11 am to 7 pm, Sun 12 noon to 6 pm
Products: Fashion

Comme des Garçons

Design: Future Systems, Rei Kawakubo

520 West 22nd Street | New York, NY 10011 | Chelsea
Phone: +1 212 604 9200
Opening year: 1999
Subway: C, E to West 23rd Street
Opening hours: Tue–Sat 11 am to 7 pm, Sun 12 noon to 6 pm, Mon closed
Products: Fashion

Dean & Deluca

Design: Jack Ceglic

560 Broadway | New York, NY 10012 | Soho
Phone: +1 212 226 6800
www.deandeluca.com
Subway: N, R to Prince Street
Opening hours: Mon–Fri 8 am to 8 pm
Products: Fine chocolates, pastry, cheese, meat, fish, prepared foods

de Vera

Design: Federico de Vera

1 Crosby Street | New York, NY 10013 | Soho
Phone: +1 212 625 0838
www.deveraobjects.com
Subway: 6, J, M, N, Q, R, W, Z to Canal Street
Opening hours: Tue–Sat 11 am to 7 pm
Products: Decorative arts, venetian glass, jewelry, Japanese lacquer

997 Madison Avenue | New York, NY 10021 | Upper East Side
Phone: +1 212 537 5000
www.fragments.com
Subway: 6 to 77th Street
Opening hours: Mon–Sat 10 am to 6 pm, Sun closed
Products: Jewelry
Special features: There is an assortment of 30 designers to choose
from at any given time

Industries Stationery

Design: Roger Hirsch Architect, Myriam Corti

91 Crosby Street | New York, NY 10012 | Soho
Phone: +1 212 334 4447
www.industriesstationery.com
Subway: R, W to Prince Street; 6 to Spring Street
Opening hours: Mon–Sat 11 am to 7 pm, Sun 12 noon to 6 pm
Products: Notecards, notebooks, journals, photo albums, Lexon and Pinetti accessories
Special features: Seasonal collections of products deliver variety and distinctive style

Jeffrey

449 West 14th Street | New York, NY 10014 | Chelsea
Phone: +1 212 206 1272
Subway: A, C, E to 14th Street; L to Eighth Avenue
Opening hours: Mon, Tue, Wed, Fri 10 am to 8 pm, Thur 10 am to 9 pm,
Sat 10 am to 7 pm, Sun 12:30 pm to 6 pm
Products: Men's and Women's clothing, shoes, accessories, cosmetics, fine jewelry

Jonathan Adler

Design: Jonathan Adler Design Team

47 Greene Street | New York, NY 10013 | Soho
Phone: +1 212 941 8950
www.jonathanadler.com
Opening year: 2003
Subway: 6 to Spring Street
Opening hours: Mon–Sat 11 am to 7 pm, Sun 12 noon to 6 pm
Products: Pottery, lighting, textiles, lacquer furniture, lacquer bath, handbags, groovy gifts

ABBY
wishes everyone bad
would just go away

GINNY
says she's not going
from the circle

ANNA
wants to wear wigs

JONATHAN
is too old
seemingly

We believe in the innate chicness of red with brown.

P!

We believe our designs are award winning even though they're never actually won any

Kirna Zabête

Design: Nick Dine

96 Greene Street | New York, NY 10012 | Soho
Phone: +1 212 941 9656
www.kirnazabete.com
Subway: R, W to Prince Street
Opening hours: Mon–Sat 11 am to 7pm, Sun 12 noon to 6 pm
Products: Balenciaga, Chloe, Lanvin, Jimmy Choo, Jean Paul Gaultier, Viktor and Rolf,
plus dog, baby, candy

La Perla

Design: Buratti Battiston

93 Greene Street | New York, NY 10012 | Soho
Phone: +1 212 219 0999
www.laperla.com
Subway: R, W to Prince Street
Opening hours: Mon–Sat 11 am to 7pm, Sun 12 noon to 6 pm
Products: Lingerie, sleepwear, ready-to-wear, swimwear

Malin+Goetz

Design: Craig Konyk

177 7th Avenue | New York, NY 10011 | Chelsea
Phone: +1 212 727 3777
www.malinandgoetz.com
Subway: 1, 9, C, E to 23rd Street
Opening hours: Mon–Fri 11 am to 8 pm, Sat 12 noon to 8 pm, Sun 12 noon to 6 pm
Products: Skin and hair care for men and women
Special features: The office doubles as a dining room at night and hosts dinner parties
that can be viewed by customers from the avenue

Miya Shoji

Design: Zui Hanafusa, Hisao Hanafusa

109 West 17th Street | New York, NY 10011 | Chelsea
Phone: +1 212 243 6774
www.miyashoji.com
Subway: 1, 2, 3, 9 to 14th Street or 1, 9 to 18th Street
Opening hours: Mon–Fri 9 am to 6 pm
Products: Custom hand crafted Japanese interiors
Special features: Two-sided shoji, tatami platforms, single slab tables, light fixtures

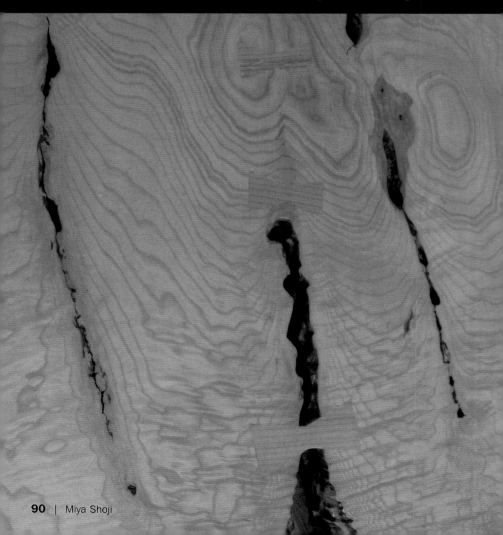

Miya Shoji

109 West 17th St.

MoMA Design and Book Store

Design: Richard Gluckman

11 West 53rd Street | New York, NY 10019 | Midtown
Phone: +1 212 708 9700
www.momastore.org
Subway: E, V to 5th Avenue; B, D, F to 47–50 Streets (Rockefeller Center)
Opening hours: Sat–Thu 9:30 am to 6:30 pm, Fri 9:30 am to 9 pm
Products: art books, modern art reproductions, design objects, gifts
Special features: The MoMA Design and Book Store features one of Manhattan's finest
selections of more than 2,000 art book titles

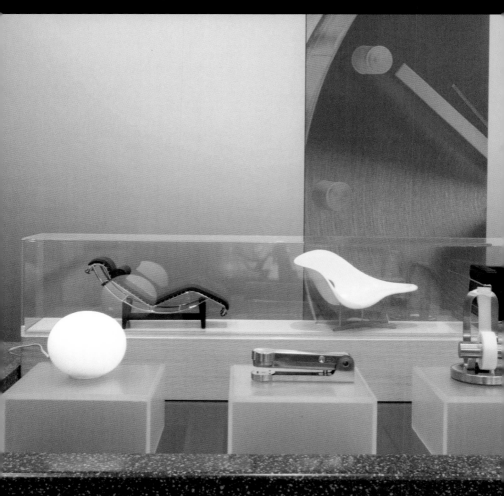

Products: furniture, lighting, watches, jewelry, books and other design pieces
Special features: Events and exhibitions at Moss

alla città"

Phone: +1 212 431 8252
www.mzwallace.com
Subway: R, W to Prince Street; 6 to Spring Street
Opening hours: Mon–Sat 11 am to 7 pm, Sun 12 noon to 6 pm
Products: Handbags
Special features: Furniture designed by Franz West

Nakedeye

Design: George Lee

192 Orchard Street | New York, NY 10002 | Lower East Side
Phone: +1 212 253 4935
Subway: F to 2nd Avenue
Opening hours: Fall / Winter Mon–Fri 1 pm to 7 pm, Sat 12 noon to 7 pm,
Sun 12 noon to 6 pm
Spring / Summer Mon–Fri 1 pm to 8 pm, Sat 12 noon to 8 pm, Sun 12 noon to 6 pm
Products: Eyeglasses, sunglasses
Special features: eye examination

Polux Fleuriste

Design: Anouchka Levy

248 Mott Street | New York, NY 10012 | Nolita
Phone: +1 212 219 9646
Opening year: 2002
Subway: B, D, F, V, 6 to Broadway-Lafayette Street or R, W to Prince Street
Opening hours: Mon–Sat 10 am to 7 pm, Sun closed
Products: Flower shop (unusual flowers), candles, books, tea, vintage products (linen, jars, bottles etc.), hand made products, baby products, cosmetics

HAND TO EARTH
Andy Goldsworthy

www.prada.com
Opening year: 2001
Subway: B, D, F, V to Broadway-Lafayette Street or R, W to Prince Street
Opening hours: Mon–Fri 11 am to 7 pm, Sun 12 noon to 6 pm
Products: Fashion

www.rby45rpm.com
Opening year: 2000
Subway: B, D, F, V to Broadway-Lafayette Street or R, W to Prince Street
Opening hours: Mon–Sat 11 am to 7 pm, Sun 12 noon to 7 pm
Products: Women's and men's casual clothing

Rizzoli Bookstore

Design: Hugh Hardy

31 West 57th Street | New York, NY 10019 | Midtown
Phone: +1 212 759 2424
www.rizzoliusa.com
Subway: F to 57th Street
Opening hours: Mon–Fri 10 am to 7:30 pm, Sat 10:30 am to 7 pm, Sun 11 am to 7 pm
Products: Books, CDs
Special features: The international clientele consider this the most beautiful bookshop in America

Silks
for the Sultans

PASSAGE

Visión de México
y sus Artistas

Visión de México
y sus Artistas

Visión de México
y sus Artistas

Sigerson Morrison

Design: Sage Wimer Coombe

28 Prince Street | New York, NY 10012 | Soho
Phone: +1 212 219 3893
www.sigersonmorrison.com
Subway: N, R to Prince Street, 6 to Spring Street
Opening hours: Mon–Sat 11 am to 7 pm, Sun 12 noon to 6 pm
Products: Shoes

The Conran Shop

Design: Conran & Partners

407 East 59th Street | New York, NY 10022 | Midtown
Phone: +1 212 755 9079
www.conran.com
Subway: 4, 5, 6 to Lexington Avenue; N, R to 59th Street
Opening hours: Mon–Fri 11 am to 8 pm, Sat 10 am to 7pm, Sun 12 noon to 6 pm
Products: Upholstery, chairs, tables, kitchen accessories, bath accessories, lighting, kids
toys, frames, books, electronics
Special features: The shop showcases an innovative design sense and the European love
of texture and warmth

Xukuma

Design: Georgia Boothe

183 Lenox Avenue | New York, NY 10026 | Harlem
Phone: +1 212 222 0490
www.xukuma.com
Subway: 2, 3 to 116th Street
Opening hours: Wed–Sun 12 noon to 7 pm
Products: Gifts, accessories, t-shirts, funky costume jewelry, bags, home decor, fashion
Special features: Store changes each season, unique one-of-a-kind gifts sourced from around the world, some evenings there is wine and jazz

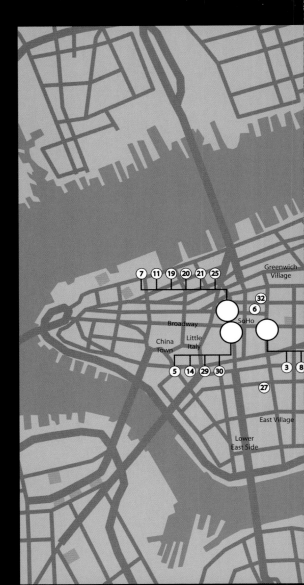

Greenwich Village

Broadway

SoHo

China Town

Little Italy

East Village

Lower East Side

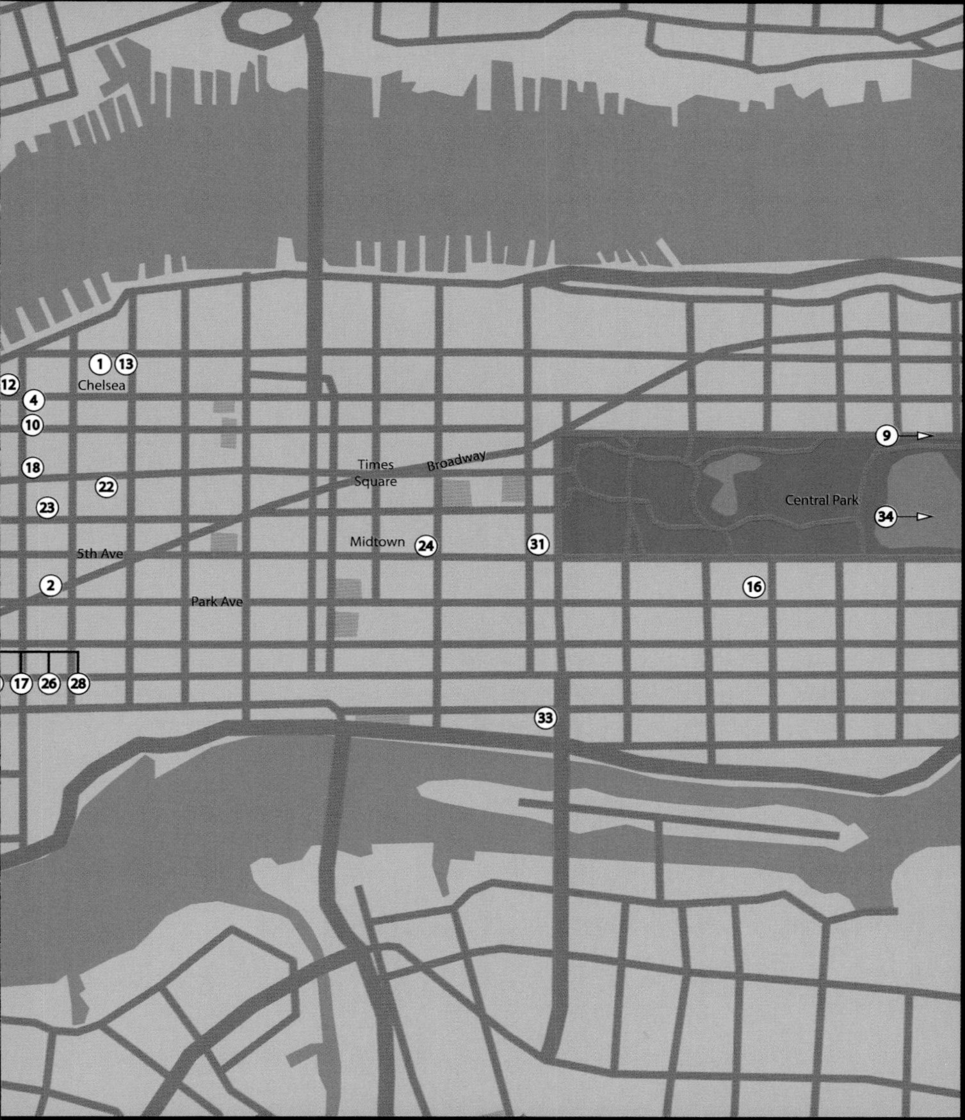
1
13
Chelsea
12
4
10
18
22
23
5th Ave
2
Park Ave
17
26
28
Times
Square
Broadway
Midtown
24
31
33
9
Central Park
34
16

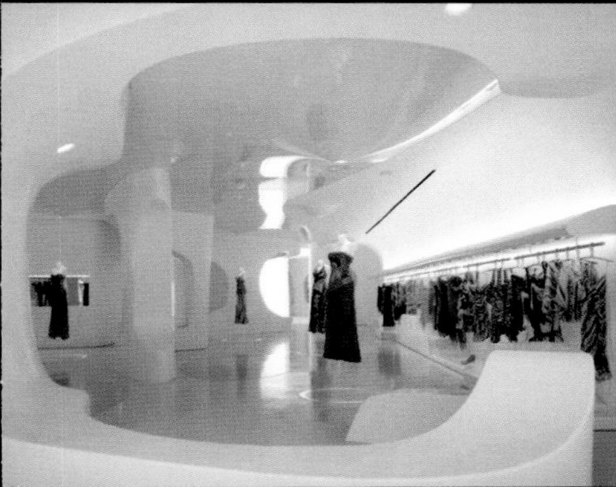

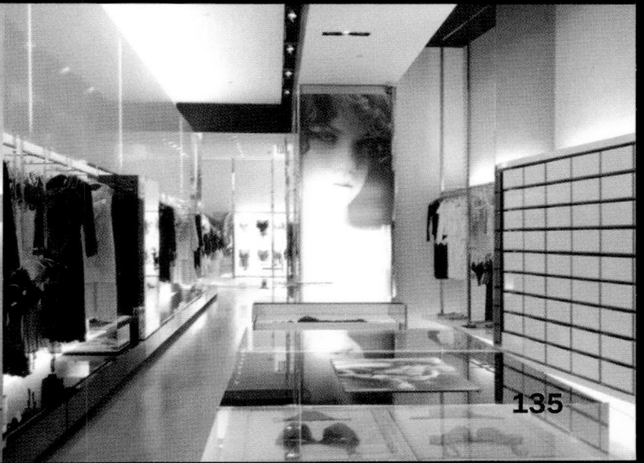

COOL SHOPS

Size: 14 x 21.5 cm / 5 $\frac{1}{2}$ x 8 $\frac{1}{2}$ in.
136 pp
Flexicover
c. 130 color photographs
Text in English, German, French,
Spanish and Italian

Other titles in the same series:

ISBN
3-8327-9073-X

ISBN
3-8327-9070-5

ISBN
3-8327-9038-1

ISBN
3-8327-9071-3

ISBN
3-8327-9022-5

ISBN
3-8327-9072-1

ISBN
3-8327-9037-3

**To be published in the
same series:**

Amsterdam
Dubai
Hamburg
Hongkong
Madrid
Miami

San Francisco
Shanghai
Singapore
Tokyo
Vienna

teNeues